AF279665

THE DAY I TURNED INTO CHLOÉ

Bibliografische Information der Deutschen Nationalbibliothek: Die Deutsche Nationalbibliothek
verzeichnet diese Publikation in der Deutschen Nationalbibliografie;
detaillierte bibliografische Daten sind im internet über http://dnb.dnb.de
abrufbar.
Die automatisierte Analyse des Werkes, um daraus Informationen insbesondere über Muster,
Trends und Korrelationen gemäß §44b UrhG („Text und Data Mining") zu gewinnen,
ist untersagt.
© 2025 Katharina Stertz
Verlag: BoD · Books on Demand GmbH, Überseering 33, 22297 Hamburg,
bod@bod.de
Druck: Libri Plureos GmbH, Friedensallee 273, 22763 Hamburg
ISBN: 978-3-8192-1169-0

Trigger Warning:
This book contains sensitive content including mental disorders (psychosis), abuse, suicide, murder, psychiatric hospital and other themes that may evoke discomfort for some readers. Please read with caution and if you believe that certain topics could be triggering for you, consider seeking support.

This book contains spoilers of my novel 'Folie à Deux'. I am giving insights into the backgrounds of the story, the characters and their connection to each other.

folie
à deux
(intro)

did
I
want
to be
with
him
or
did
I
want
to be
like
him?

spring
one year ago
the day I turned into Chloé
someone who only exists
in my imagination
an invention
another version
of myself

am I even real
today is the first time
I think about death again
am I even real
if I see death as compassion

am I even real
that I believe
only an idol
a person I don't know
I have never met in my life
a person I desired to become
could save me from death

no one believes me
I swear this is the truth
this is the realest thing about me
he is the reason why I live a little bit longer
than I should have
he is the reason I am still alive

whenever I thought about dying
he was there
even if he only exists in my head
does it mean I saved myself
am I even real

the day I turned into chloé

I am very bad with choosing names for my characters. I know beautiful names but I associate them with the wrong people. I had some small test perfumes in my drawer. One of them was by Chloé. I thought 'what a beautiful name for a book character'. I loved the sound of the name, the colours of the letters and the scent of the perfume of course. The *idea* of her character was born long ago and then came her name. I spontaneously put the perfume on before I went to a concert of my favourite artist I used to be obsessed with. I believed I could get closer to her, to her world. It was the day I turned into Chloé.

'Folie à Deux'
I want to share my life with you
you have dreams
and I have insanity
enough for us two
being crazy alone is boring
so be my partner in crime
I have a broken soul
so let me break yours, too

I have a broken soul
so let me break yours, too

'Folie à Deux' (ICD-10 F24.0) means 'shared madness', 'delusion for two', as if a psychosis could be contagious. Luc is losing his mind over fame and recognition. Chloé is losing her mind over Luc. Victor is losing his mind over Chloé. Everything is happening twice like an echo. It s a reference to the number two because Chloé is going through everything twice. First with Luc, then with Victor who are also symbolising two opposites and yet they manage to mirror her in the same way. She is stuck in a loop. Like in a never ending repeating karmic cycle.

The story plays in Paris, the city of love, but love doesn't exist in this story. That's why I used French names. And it's matching that the name of this mental disorder was French, too. Chloé just wants to be admired. She maybe loved Luc wholeheartedly, but if you look closer, she just did it because he was famous, well-known and popular. She only loved a picture, the idea of him. If he had been a lonely, poor artist, she wouldn't even have looked into his direction. Also, we don't know if Luc really loved Chloé or just performed. And Victor was holding onto Chloé because he wanted to 'heal' her. However, she manipulates him because she wanted him to become a copy of Luc, to make her idol 'more available' for her.

On top of this, everyone is experiencing their own kind of psychosis or delusion, symbolising the hidden depths of the one's psyche. Chloé suffers from amorous paranoia, believing that her idol Luc and her were meant for each other. Luc gets paranoid that he is being stalked or followed by his fans, working until reaching a state of burn out. Victor believes that Chloé was meant to enter his life to save him. On the other hand he thinks that every artist is insane in some way which makes him believe that Chloé needs help.

In all chaos there is a cosmos, in all disorder a secret order.

the
cosmos
is
just
chaos
making
sense

there are those
visions
in my head
and I don't know
if those are real
predictions
or my own
wishes

I have seen you
even if I didn't know
how you looked like
I heard melodies
in my head
that didn't exist
and you made them
real

**I forgot his name
but the impression he left stayed forever**

The idea of 'Folie à Deux' started when I was watching the movie 'based on a true story', adapted from the novel by Delphine de Vigan. It s about how the character L. broke into Delphine s life. It started very subtly, turned into a toxic dependency. Especially the scene where L. dyed her hair gave me the idea.

I had visions of the characters in my head. An obsessed fan, an idol and someone else looking similar to the idol of the story but having a completely different personality. A story about manipulation and dependency.

How far can you go by changing someone s personality? Can you be happy with someone who reminds you of someone else?

he was the first one
and my last
always lingering in the back of my head
I forgot his name
but the impression he left stayed forever
something magically familiar
like it belonged to me
it flowed down
like the water
down in the hole of my sink
will we ever meet again, I asked
not knowing whom I meant
flickering on tv
looking through him
like he was invisible
I was thirteen years old
I heard about people having celebrity crushes
it's the dumbest thing someone could ever have
I am not like that
I will never be like that
I promise
I am not dumb
 cause I know
they don t know
I exist
and I couldn t prevent myself from falling
the boys at school all knew me
I just wanted to seem invisible
every year someone else
I turned fourteen
and all I wanted was a rich man
I did not believe in soulmates
forgot what happened last year
like amnesia
there is a familiar face
I cannot recognise
I just chase good looking men
from now on

collecting them like coins
even if I know I am invisible for them
and I will never have a chance
it was only about admiration
just idols on the stage I couldn t reach
I was happy
they didn t know I existed
I always wished to never exist
but deep down I knew it was a role I played
we are so similar I said
interviews were instructions
what to like or not to like
like a chameleon I adapted myself
I hated myself so much
I wanted to be someone else
I believed no one will ever love me
for who I was
to please or not to be liked back
that s the question
I knew I will replace them one day
later my eyes are stuck on someone else
my next victim I can only see on my phone
I just switch it off when I have enough
but the first one was always there
like a faded memory of a dream
secretly I was looking for him
somewhere

there was this
woman on the train
in a different country
drawing portraits
in her sketchbook
I don't know why
I remember this moment
so clearly
everyone was looking
at their phones
and my eyes were stuck on her
I wanted to be like her
I could totally picture myself
becoming her
she seemed so peaceful
just her making art
doing what she loved
artists are just children
who refused to grow up
I wanted to do
what I wanted, too

venus ruled person
not able to find love

my love to art is stronger
than my love to people

I love love
but love doesn't love me back

I love love but love doesn't love me back

The hardest parts of writing Folie à Deux were the romantic relationship scenes, seeing everything through rose coloured glasses. I have never been in a romantic relationship, never experienced the feeling of loving someone and being loved back by them. Others think it's weird, but for me, it's not a bad thing, I have been living like this, I got used to it. Everyone follows different aims and dreams in life. But writing those scenes really felt like I was lying to the readers. I don t know how a romantic relationship works. I wanted to create a lovely, romantic atmosphere, then I was wondering: 'is this really what couples do?' 'is this how they feel?' 'Is that awkward?' Of course, I can watch romance movies, I can read books, but I never experienced it on my own, I never felt it so how was I supposed to describe those feelings? So it was really hard to put it into words.

divorce is a sin
and marriage
was a theatre play
just written for me
one day she stopped
wearing her ring
the show is over
the curtain closes

I wanted to get married one day
white dress and roses
till death do us apart
golden ring on my finger
promising me forever

there's no person beside me

what kind of guys
are you into?
she asks me
blonde, I say
it just blurted out
and I don t know why
it doesn t make sense
because I am not even
into blondes
and blue eyes?
she asks
it feels off
I can t see anything
in my imagination
there is a black and white video in my mind
not knowing where it's coming from
and I can t think of anyone else
as if my fantasy wasn't able
to imagine another face
someone I just invented
just him

can you fall in love with someone
you have never met?

I am happier alone than with someone else
I could never love sincerely

maybe I wasn't meant to love
I was meant to achieve my goals

they warn me about ending up lonely
but I am not scared

Victor is different, shy, cautious, looking like a loner but no one understands that he actually enjoys spending time alone. I believe that he is very sensitive, very easy to influence or manipulate because deep down he cares too much what others might think of him. He tries to distance himself from the others, from other people's views and opinions. Then, he started feeling 'different' since people told him he was weird for not finding his 'other half'. That s why he lets Chloé walk over him. He is a huge people pleaser, so am I. Slowly, he started to be scared of not being liked by others even if he deeply knows that it s not healthy for him. And I am not sure if he really loved Chloé or if he just played along because he was so unbearably lonely. Like Luc he is obsessed with his goals and his achievements to distract himself from his feelings but in a different font.

I learnt to be scared of intimacy
I learnt that people who love you the most
will hurt you the most
they never meant to harm me
but it s not good for me
the biggest haters are not on the internet
I am sharing a home with them

I built my own fantasy world in my head
to protect myself from the cold outside
they say make your mind a place to be
but you are delusional
if you spend too much time there

I lie to survive
I write to escape
I describe my dreams
as if they were real
sometimes the lines between
reality and fiction
blur and blend
I am the unreliable narrator
inventing something nonexistent
yes, I lie to survive

wake up from your fantasy world
they say
stop taking all those things away from me
that used to make me happy
stop breaking all the things
I try to build

I don t want to wake up
I didn t mean to harm myself

they say
love yourself first, the right person will come
as if it was so easy
no one will love you if you hate yourself

I started to love myself so much
that I didn't need another person to complete me

some people hate themselves so much
they can't stand to be alone with their own thoughts
while I love getting lost in my own world

but why do people get the most love
who hate themselves the most?

look at me
please look at me
I'm here

I can understand Chlo'és obsession with a phantom, her desire to be loved by someone she can t actually have. Striving for something that isn t real, that isn't achievable. That s her way to escape reality, instead of coping with her real problems. She has everything she wanted but she doesn t feel seen or heard. From her feeling of loneliness and her low self worth, she started to believe that her idol, someone who doesn t know her, was her soulmate or someone similar to her just to feel pride. She wanted to show off being the lover of a star, of a celebrity. As if she shouts: *Look at me. Look, how close he is. Look, who knows me. Look, who loves me.*

people talk
about love
and romance
all the time
it's better than
complaining
but they are
making you feel
like you are
no one
without it
like there is
something
missing
in your life
the last puzzle
but it's okay
it's valid
if you don't have it
it's okay
if you don't
strive for that
but you will never know
what real luck feels like
why don't you talk
about your dreams
about yourself instead

they make you feel
that you don't deserve love
if you don't work for it
but that's not how it works

where do they go to find love
like a foreign land
too far away from me

love happens
it happens so effortlessly
for me it never happened
and it never will
the universe forgot me
I don't see myself with
someone by my side

no one ever had
a crush on me
so I start to believe
that I am unloveable
like there is something wrong
or broken
if you spend too much time alone

I always wanted
to make art and write
why can't they just understand
I am walking a different path

I am not a woman
without a man
I am not a woman
if I don't want children
I am not
I am no one
I am nothing
I swallow their words like it's poison

they warn me about
ending up lonely
but I am not scared
I love myself so much
no one can give me the love
that I can give to myself

so much love inside
I don't know
who I should give it to
I can't carry it anymore

I never wanted romance
it looks so staged
drama and fights
a waste of time
but there is so much
art about love
all those songs on the radio
were about love
and I never related to them
movies on tv are all about love
and I am crying when
there is a happy ending
because I never knew
how they are feeling
and I will never be able
to feel the same things
am I still an artist
if I can't see the beauty
in romance?

since I am thirteen
I am ashamed if someone asks me
if I have a crush
I am looking up to men on tv
maybe there is something wrong with me
obsessing over people who don't know me
and I know I will
never have a chance
I just admire them
like they are versions of people
I could become one day
if I worked on myself
but I never wanted to be seen

I knew this was not real
I knew they didn t know me
and they didn t know how I looked like
how could they dislike me
if they didn t know I exist

I am fifteen years old
my classmates have their first cheesy relationships
you have no time to think about boys
if you are worried about your future
sometimes I invented a crush from school
and when I really crushed on someone
it disappeared after some days
and sometimes I was wondering
if I was into girls

since I am seventeen years old
I want to marry a rich and famous man
I would be the woman waiting for him at home
and no one would ever know
as if I have access to the backstage
to corners no one has ever seen
give me money and I give you admiration

I am eighteen and something seems off
what if I lied to myself all the time
do I really want to know how it feels like to be loved
or is it their voices saying
it's so weird such a pretty girl like you
doesn't have a boyfriend
what if there is no one out there for me
I fell in love with a fantasy instead
mum, I love him but he isn't real

and yet I romanticise love
but when I imagine to kiss someone
I flinch
I shudder when I think about
how other people imagine me
I don't need anyone to be complete

I thought I was never good enough
now I start thinking no one is good enough for me

when I listen to other people
talking about love and relationships
I feel like a child sitting at the table
with adults who talk about things
I can t understand
I am getting older
and I am wondering
if this feeling ever disappears

I never cried over a heartbreak or over boys
I cried for shame and exposure
I cried for my future
my tears were filled
with worries and anxiety of the future
filled with anger and frustration
of being different
of never being good enough

I am thinking about success instead
but success is not thinking about me
and they say I should love myself more
yes, I love myself
but I don t love myself back

138 258 56
Will i ever be good enough?

the
quiet
girl
from
school
is
famous
now

I got the
most love
when
I hated
myself
the most

I want
those
heart
shaped
likes
on my screen
the reward
for giving up
my identity
give me more
feed me with
more
artificial love
and dopamine
until I forget
myself
until I forget
who I used
to be

I want to be famous
until I forget that I hate myself

I think the book is talking about the shame of being truly
yourself, playing another role for others because you hate
yourself. Everyone is performing. Luc on the stage. Chloé
for Luc. Victor for Chloé. Wearing masks, terrified of their
own reflections.

138 258 56
204 511 138
1

she has so many followers
ten-thousand, they say
twelve-thousand, I correct
it's not even a lot

I am on a party with people from school
I was drunk from alcohol
I watch them smoke weed
and I had an overdose of pride instead
they call me an influencer
but compared to them I am nothing
at school they are looking up to me
just because of a number on my page
teachers knew that
and the message got spread
they looked at me with different eyes
the quiet girl at school is famous on the internet
my words are famous
but not my face

they call me an influencer
I only made memes for fun
for my own amusement
I read the stars
I read their astrology charts
they want me to talk about them
no one wanted to know about mine

I see my friend flirting with boys older than her
I drag her away from them
I never knew what love felt like
there was only love on my screen
only superficial crushes
one day I will marry a rich man, I believe
or I become a rich man on my own
who needs love if you can have external validation
anonymous numbers on my screen
why should I date one man
if I get attention of thousands of them

they call me an influencer
you can make money out of that
I monetise spirituality
I am selling the secrets of the stars
it felt so wrong
because I made it just for entertainment
what if they were right
and I never needed to work anymore
I sold cheap jewellery
money ruins friendships
for the first time I understood what it meant
just because of a number
they thought I was cool
and I wanted more
selling merchandise
and more
getting drunk by likes
I want to be so famous
until I forget that I hate myself

and the dumber and superficial the memes get
the more attention I receive
work smart not hard
it feels so wrong but I keep going
because I'm never satisfied
and I need more

they call me an influencer
I was only seventeen
and I lived such a different life
school and homework like everyone else
making memes at night
like a drug addict who refuses to recover
I don't know anything about life
if I lock myself in my dark room
entertaining the crowd
receiving compliments in return

my phone is blowing up
but where are my real friends?

just do it for the chase for dopamine
my eyes get wider
and I feel like I am worth something again
when the words I wrote found meaning

when you were up there in the clouds
one day you will crash down
until nothing is left behind the screen
hype is never forever
tomorrow you will be forgotten
phone is silent
and no one can fill my inner void
anymore

I want to turn my life
into a dream
I don t need sleep
I need to stay awake
and write more
my love to art is unconditional
and if you sleep you stop loving
if life gives you lemons
squeeze them until nothing is left
I don t deserve sleep
not yet

**if life gives you lemons
squeeze them until nothing is left**

Luc is also a very toxic person in my novel who is even scarier and more disturbing than Chloé. Chloé is losing herself for a man she can t have. Luc is losing himself and his identity for admiration, for fame, for reputation. And he is ready to give everything up. He is ready to cross boundaries, to abuse his power for admiration. And it's scary if you realise, how far he was ready to go to get more. He is that kind of person who is never satisfied so he ends up looping, too.

I used to overwork myself, too, abusing and taking my health for granted until I couldn't do normal tasks or not understanding what was happening around me anymore.

Money and fame can blind you even more than falling in love for someone toxic or unavailable. I distracted the reader into believing that Chloé is a danger to herself because of her toxic obsession. But actually, it's Luc who is the menace.

So be careful who you put on a pedestal, you never know who your idols really are.

who needs love
if you can have external validation?

Chloé is scared of being like everyone else. She wanted to be special, to be better than everyone else, to make everyone jealous of her. Luc is a trophy, an achievement she wants to reach. She doesn t love, she only wants appreciation, being the centre of attention, being in the lime light without being a star. And she is scared of losing. Scared of losing Luc because he is the only thing that keeps her alive.

this is my last release day
one last time being the only one listening
to my own song on midnight alone in my room
it's dark here and my phone shines on my face

release days are like birthdays
I see who is caring about me

one last time of feeling lonely and worthless

one last time seeing how strangers care more
than my own friends
I see, they are awake, too
not writing a single word
I wish they were jealous instead
it would seem like they cared

one last time seeing how those hopes
turn into disappointment

one last time remembering how our dreams
never got realised

one last time feeling like the loneliest in this world
I am no one without contacts

one last time noticing how everyone forgets
their favourite artists started small one day, too
but it was never cool to support small artists
I wanted to be one of them
but not everyone can make it
they stopped believing in me
so I stopped believing in myself
I wish external validation
wasn't that important to me
so I could love myself even more
first time I am happy it's over

give me money and I give you admiration

I wanted to be Chloé because she gained lots of money from her art, from something she loved, she could waste it as if it was unlimited. I strived for money and wealth as if it could replace my wish of being loved so I rather wanted to become rich and hyper successful as if it could fill my inner void. Love was never stable because it's not material. You can say or write 'I love you' but never mean it. And money doesn't lie.

Money is not everything in life but it makes your life so much easier. If you ever struggled with money, you know what I mean.

Of course, it can t buy health, nor love nor luck. And Chloé symbolises it: her mansion is her comfort zone, she can afford everything she wanted but it doesn't fulfil her. She feels like being suffocated in gifts, in luxury products. All she ever wanted was just a song about her, a poem, a little sentence that proves that she is loved by someone. On the other side, she tries to 'buy' Victor by spoiling him with gifts, deeply knowing that it's not real love. That she found a money bill on the street before meeting him to give it to him, was a small hint as if she 'payed' to talk to him.

the tower is my tarot birth card
but will I ever get used
to those tower moments?
everything I am building up
is always collapsing
like a house of cards
there are ashes around me
I need to start from scratch and rise up
but it gets exhausting to do it
all again
no, I can t do this one more time
or I will fall apart
I tried my best
and sometimes
even the best is not enough
and while I am here sitting with my phone
I am watching others living life
travelling the world
and I wasted my youth finding myself
colours flashing on my display
in my mind it s getting darker
and in the void
he showed up
flash of light in my darkness
and the limelight was shining on him
I needed to lose everything to see you
everything needed to fade into the background
so he became the centre of attention
as if my cries for help were heard
I used to be a mirror for everyone
and he is the first one mirroring me
it seemed so staged
it couldn t be a coincidence
but what if it was a miracle

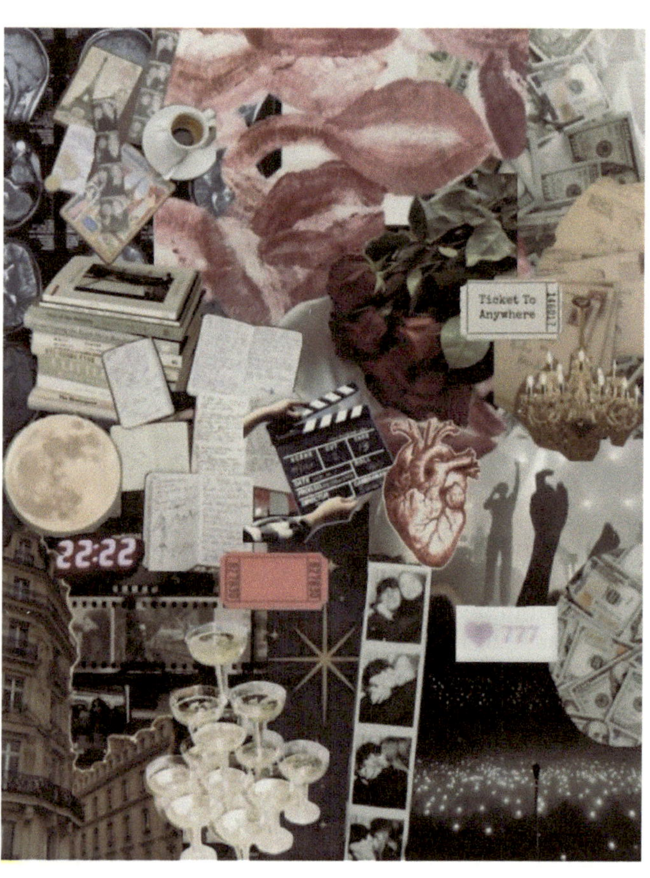

Ticket To Anywhere
22:22
777

they say
the heart wants
what it wants
but if you fall
for a celebrity
you are totally
insane

Chloé would have shouted at me:
he loves you back
he is present
he has always been there
you just can t see it
but it doesn't mean
that it's not real
if you can feel it
why don't you listen to me??

I am her creator
and even I forget that she is not real

When did I realise that Chloé was becoming me? I think it was me who turned into her. I needed to be her, to see the world through her eyes so I could write the story about her madness as if I told my own story. I wanted to show the danger of obsession because similar things happened to me. While writing 'Folie à Deux' I felt like an actor playing someone s role but I wanted to make it deceptively real until I lost myself in her. I needed to plunge in her world, in her mind, to tell the world about how she lost her mind and that s how I almost lost mine.

we
don't
know
each
other
and
we
never
will
maybe
we
are
similar
but
we
live
in
two
different
worlds

**it was only about admiration
just idols on the stage I couldn t reach**

Luc is the embodiment of power, influence, abuse, toxicity, he is the stranger people put on a pedestal randomly. A flawless shining star on the outside, a mysterious shadow behind the scenes, symbolising the darkest parts of his mind no one is allowed see. He is the brightest and the darkest character of the story.

Me, as his creator, I don't know Luc, too. No one knows Luc. He isn't just unavailable for Chloé, he is untouchable for everyone else. You either see him as a caring man or an abuser, just versions from Chloé's mind. No one knows how he is in real life because we only see him on billboards. But Luc was real. The connection between him and Chloé wasn t.

I remember
the impression
you left on me

I remember
that I have seen you

I remember
this familiarity
even if we never talked

exactly five years later
I found you again

like I was wishing
to find you

I guess you
were the person
I really needed then

like the universe showed me
that you were the person
I was praying for

you were the person
from my visions

just this song
in a language I don't speak

and yet I understand every single word
as if I wrote it myself

what if it was written about me

she was rather grieving for her sanity

Chloé never healed. She is her own enemy. Her obsession consumes her, devours her until nothing is left.

she wasn't grieving
that she lost him
or lost the connection
between them
she started grieving when she realised
it all was just an illusion
she was rather grieving for her sanity
because in that moment she was ashamed
of talking to pictures every day
ashamed of believing
that someone unreachable
someone not on her level
was her soulmate
candles around her
one last time
her feelings are burning
until they burn her down

I have insanity enough for us two

The scene that healed me, was mentioning my thoughts in Chloé's and Victor's notes in their notebooks as hidden easter eggs. I thought: Now I can say *everything* that was going on in the darkest corners of my own mind, no matter how disturbing, how unhinged it gets , expressing their feelings of despair, their attachment issues, her questions whether her idol was meant for her, whether her feelings for him were real or invented, which was also a part of me. My despair, my attachment issues. It felt like I could finally release all my feelings I once had, I used to bottle up, my confusion about what was real and what was illusion. I could finally put them on paper.

you two would look cute together
they say
I shouldn t say it
they say
and I say
yes you shouldn t say it
because I don t believe you
that s not real I think
otherwise
please tell me more
please feed my delusions
I need more and more
until they explode again

I feel like
falling over and over again
I am falling for the unseen
for the secrets no one can see
for the man behind the fame
I fall in love with the version
I invented in my head

he loves me

he loves me not

he loves me

he loves me not

I just lost count

I love him

I love him not

I love him

because he is like me

I love him not

because he is like me

I love myself

but I don't love myself back

I just find him aesthetically pleasing
like a portrait in a gallery I stare at
I know I shouldn't touch it
and I don't want to
and I don't want to be touched
I want to be someone's artwork, too

I want to take him home
hang him on the wall
and stare at him like in a gallery
no one else can see it
no one else can take it away from me

I want to be someone's artwork, too

I can understand Chloé's longing for understanding. Her biggest wish was to experience mutual love. She admires and wants to be admired back. Luc is her muse and she wants to be his. She is doing anything for him and wants him to do anything for her back.

you are my statue
I created a version
of you in my head
cold
made of stone
and I am wishfully waiting for you
to become alive

how could they dislike me
if they didn t know I exist

What does it mean to love someone who doesn t know you exist? Is it still love? Is it a safer way? It s not love. I think true love is mutual. But loving someone who doesn t know you exist is safer because you are aware that they can t hurt you. You can create a whole love story in your fantasy. The only thing that may hurt is, that you are lying to yourself by believing that made up love story in your head. You believe that you are protecting yourself from being vulnerable while you realise that you are not able to love and to be loved.

the rain was
falling down
we were walking together
under my umbrella
you held my arm
the way you looked at me
confused me
the day was perfect
but I spent it with the
wrong person

I never belong anywhere
and I believed I belonged to you

People say opposites attract but I wanted to show the toxic side of that. Chloé and Victor embody the things the other hates. Victor hates artists. Chloé hates doctors. I wanted to create a huge contrast, like two opposites mirroring their wounds to each other. Also if you compare Victor to Luc they are looking alike but also result as opposites if you dig deeper. Luc is deceitful by showing himself as a flawless star, seeming like he is better, more successful than everyone else, bragging with his wealth and being admired by everyone around him. On the other side, Victor is symbolising someone who feels like never being good enough, misunderstood, hardworking and jealous of other people achieving more than him. He is the embodiment of losing his identity to please others or to be accepted. He symbolises the fear of not really belonging anywhere because of being too different.

you
are not
me
and
I
am not
you
and
I
will never be
you

I think I should
believe
that there is
someone else
meant for me
waiting for me
even though
I rather want
to be alone
than with
someone else
who is not you
you were
the person
I was waiting for
and I don't know
if you are waiting
for someone
like me, too
now I just
want to know
how to love
someone
who loves
me back
I want to know
how it feels like
to be loved
by someone
I love
I wished to be
saved by you
but I saved myself

I cry and I feel their eyes on me
why did this happen to me

Actually, I didn t see it coming that Luc abused Chloé. It just happened by writing. It s kinda metaphorical because you can never know if it may happen to you one day, too. You never know how people really tick until they drop their masks and you never know when they show their true colours.

I wanted to show how much Chloé's delusion hurts her by making Luc physically abusing her. The most hurtful part is Chloé's awareness that she should leave him but she refuses, she doesn t want to because her love to him blinded her so much.

I always wanted
a famous partner
I would get money
and recognition instead
if I didn t know
how love actually felt like
I only knew these butterflies
in my stomach
could never survive
I wanted to be
in the limelight, too
no one would see
my shadow
and I was wondering
is there someone out there
whom I don t need
to change myself for
whom I could recognise
myself in
like in a mirror
I used to break it every time
now he makes me
put the cracks together
now I am talking to the stars
every night saying:
'*I wish he wasn t famous*'

**like a mirror I used to break every time
now he makes me put the cracks together**

The only difference between Chloé and me is, that she loves her idol because of his fame and talent. I fell for my favourite artist because he reminded me of myself so much like I was looking in a mirror. And I would have felt in the same if he hadn't been famous.

mostly
I really
wonder
why this
happened
what kind of
lecture
this was
why did the
universe
send me
someone
I couldn't
have
someone
who could never
love me back
someone
I could never
reach
no matter
how much
I grow

I am not Chloé - I made it out - but she didn't

If I could talk to Chloé, I would advise her to enjoy life, to see the beauty in the small things in life. I feel like she is missing out on real life while living in her fantasy all the time. And I think it s scary how far her escapism goes until it s turning into insanity she can t escape of. She is making her mind a nice place to be until it turns into a prison.

I
was believing
in you
in us
2
for a
long time
I believed
that all
those things
between us
could not
be just
coincidences

I thought you were meant for me

                    and I was meant for you

but you were only meant

                    to find myself again

when things were falling apart

                    I know we are soulmates

but we aren't meant to be

                    maybe in another universe

we are together

I used to see you in my dreams
felt like we met in another dimension

The mirrored room scene was inspired of a vision I had in 2022, it was a dream I had. This scene is exactly in the middle of the book, carrying lots of symbolic meaning. It s right after Chloé's down spiral and right before waking up in reality that she tried too hard to escape from, like a break, a transition. It was the peak of Chloé's delusion: she just dances with Luc in a room full of mirrors and lights, with that person who is basically just mirroring her. Just the two of them and infinity. Her delusion is multiplying and repeating over and over again in the next chapters.

But this scene is a peaceful moment, as if time stops, a little unrealistic trial how it felt to be close to him. As if her wish is becoming real in a rebirth moment. It looked aesthetically pleasing in my mind, but we shouldn t forget that Luc is the embodiment of someone who destroyed her, who affected her perception.

You may think that he is the villain in her story, but actually it s her own delusion. And the atmosphere in the mirror room makes it deceitful, looking like a dream you don t want to wake up from, followed by a plot twist: Out of the blue, he lets her go and says: 'we will meet again very soon. I promise', a hint that soulmates always find their way and will always be connected with each other, no matter if you want it or not. It s a little foretaste of what may happen in the next chapters.

"I'm not crazy. My reality is just different than yours."
Before Alice got to Wonderland, she had to fall.

my
mind
played
tricks
on
me
and
I
played
along

time is an illusion and yet I hear the clock ticking

I think there is a very fine line between obsession and delusion. Obsession means, that you can t live without something, you are dependent on something, on digging deeper, on finding answers. You make it dominate your life. You make everything about one person. You live only for that person. But still you can differ reality from delusion. Delusion means, believing in something that isn t real. Believing someone loves you back who doesn t actually love you. And then you try to find answers if the voices in your head are right or not while the lines blur. Maybe it s the way how we cope with it. Creating out of obsession saved me from delusion.

I feel like Alice
falling for you
was like falling into the rabbit hole
drinking the drink-me potion
eating the eat-me cake
and see, I am growing and shrinking
like my mood swings
I am too big
the chess board floor
looks so small under my feet
between black and white squares
and sometimes I am too small
for this world
I never belong anywhere
and I believed I belonged to you
I hear the walls talking to me
the furniture is making fun of me
and I am wondering
if this will ever end
I fall deeper until
I cannot trust my perception
anymore
time is an illusion
and yet I hear the clock ticking
I know those things
I am hearing and seeing
are not real
and I go deeper
until I ask myself
am I even real

I know
it s all
invented
and I
lied to you
until I
believed
my own lies
I just played
tricks on you like
my mind played
tricks on me
and I played along
I wanted
to get over it
because I knew
it lead me to nothing
or do I want
to get over
because they
expect me to do so
and now they
lock me up
because
I told them
the truth

'*wow, we have a gifted artist here*'
I say *thank you*, focused on my drawing
'*where did you learn to draw like that?*'
'*at school*'
I keep scribbling pink tulips on my paper
it s spring and I am at hospital
flowers are blooming outside
but it's still winter in the therapy rooms
the therapist says
we should show our pictures
and I showed them mine
I felt awkward
astonished faces around me
at school they said that art
should only be a hobby for me
I am good but not good enough
and I will never be enough

I used
to see
you
in my
dreams
felt like
we
met
in another
dimension
I thought
this is
forever
now there are
pills
in my body
chemicals
etching
you
away
I stay
awake
because
you
are
missing

fifth grade
and we are sitting in a circle
two women in the middle talking about drugs
to prevent us from them
don t take drugs or you get psychosis
someone raised his hand
'what does psychosis mean?
'a person who is suffering from psychosis
sees or hears things that don t exist
like spiders climbing on his arms
but no one else can see them'
I imagined someone
in a cell of a mental institution
red spiders climbing on his arms
he is screaming
but no one knows why he is scared
I was scared of taking drugs
my parents protected me from them
I never used them
and yet it happened to me
I was going through a horror trip
without abusing drugs
therapy room
and we are sitting in a circle
I cry and I feel
their eyes on me
why did this happen to me

my fantasy world is like
a closed amusement park
it feels like I am looking
at the words
like pictures
with no meaning
my life stopped
while the world
keeps turning

my fantasy world is like a closed amusement park

Before I started therapy, I bought *his* book. It wasn't written in my mother tongue so it was very difficult for me to understand. Additionally, I took pills that relieved my symptoms. I got sedated. My movements got slower. My thoughts got slower. I felt like just staring at words with no meaning. And no one understood who the author was. I had no feelings to him but still I wanted to try to read his book. It was weird that I was at a hospital, reading a book written by someone whom I almost lost my mind over. And no one got the hint who he was or what he meant to me.

One year later, when I could quit my medication, I read the book again. I could follow the plot, read between the lines and I started to find parallels to my own texts, similar sentences even if the plots were completely different. I underlined the lines that spoke to me. They were like versions of my own notes or thoughts that I wrote somewhere down.

they take drugs
to be happy
to become like me
I take them to become normal
to become like everyone else
I lived in your nightmares
voices singing me a lullaby
stumbling through the streets
drugged up with medication
it s July and my world is getting colder

my head is in the clouds
I don t need drugs
my brain is doing that on its own
the real psychos
are wearing white coats
their life goes on
mine got interrupted
I see the world keeps turning
but for me time stopped
I lost everything
it all runs like sand
through my hands
my freedom
my hopes
my dreams
in a hourglass

I look in the mirror
what have you done to me?
the colours faded
the sparkle in my eyes disappeared
and no one could repair
my broken mind
do you really think
you can heal me with drugs?

cold and empty
waiting room
smelling like
antipsychotics
and illness
like false hopes
whispering
the prognosis is good
how does it work
if it s incurable
pink coloured paper
like
rose coloured glasses
small dose
of medication
on the table
in front of me
there is no cure
for an incurable illness
this paper is a lie
that I will be fine
and I need to lie back
that I m fine

it starts again and you can't switch it off and it starts

this story
still continues
tomorrow
it will be over
tomorrow
will be feel like
yesterday
it starts
over and over
again
like a song
on repeat
until you know
the words
and the melody
by heart
you listen until
you can't
stand it
it starts
again and
you can't
switch it off
and it starts
again and again
and again
and
again
a n d
a g a i n
a n d
a g a i n
a n d
a g a i n
a n d
a g a i n
a n d

there
is
a
very
fine
line
between
twelfth
house
synastry
and
psychosis

we are soulmates but we aren't meant to be

Yes, I had an episode in my life when I truly believed that *he* was my soulmate. It was very hurtful because I knew he will never feel the same but this episode was transforming and life changing on the other side. First, when I discovered him, I believed it was just a very strange phase or a huge coincidence but the more I read or listened the more shocking it got. No one else was that similar to me like him. I used to have many idols but *he* was different. It was like there was another version of myself out there. I found more and more parallels, similarities between us. And even other people noticed it. It was eerie. So I got scared. I got paranoid. I felt how my life changed since I found him. I started to make art after I wanted to give it up, I learnt to heal, to love myself, to do the things I loved. Then, I was looking for answers why him, why it happen to me like this. It seemed so bizarre, not from this world. I read a lot about soulmates, twin flames, soul contracts. I dug deeper, obsessively collected proof and answers that he could be *the one*. And yet I still doubted it because I never met him. Why would a *celebrity* like me back. I still don t know him personally. We aren t friends or acquaintances. The version of him I am seeing in the media was maybe just a small part of him. I can t see what is happening behind the scenes. What if he is very different than I imagined him to be? I tried to distract myself, looking for someone else. I even met someone who looked like him. I got rejected but *he* always came back to me whenever I wanted to let go. In my dreams, through symbols and even in real life. And I don't know where I would be now without him. And without him, my novel 'Folie à Deux' would have never existed.

I check your zodiac sign
all your planets
I know them by heart
just to see if we match
I check the forecast
and the horoscopes
collecting answers
when we will
meet again
I know I fell for
false promises
the cosmos is just chaos
making sense
and I look for a place
to fit in

red string of fate
I am tangled in
threads cutting my skin
red like blood
I am the beginning
you are the end
I am strangling myself
I want to cut it
but I am cutting myself
I can t escape
we are connected

I can't escape we are connected

I loved the theory of the red string of fate. Everything is connected with each other. Chloé can t explain her strong pull to Luc, that s why she is believing in a connection between them two. Without him she wouldn t have made art. We don t know where she would be without her art. And without Luc she wouldn t have noticed Victor. Luc keeps following and haunting her wherever she goes. It keeps going on and on as she fails to learn her life lessons: self love and expressing gratitude.

it s Chloé
speaking to me
I follow her blindly
her voice is sweet
like sweet wine
she hypnotises me
as she casted
a powerful love spell
every syllable
is guiding me
to his direction
he is the one
she says
her voice is echoing
in my mind
I am her creator
and even I forget
that she is not real
my head is her home
I was waiting for her
to come back
so I could write about her
now I can t get rid of her
she is too similar to me
like she is a close friend
another version of myself
believe me
I hear her whispering
don t listen to the others
you are not crazy
they are just blind
they cannot see
what s real
and if I am
an illusion
so are you

writing letters to you

                        feels like writing letters to myself

I loved you the most

            because you reminded me of myself the most

you were meant to enter my life

                        so I could learn to heal

and fall in love with myself

don't you recognise me?
I am your biggest fan and you don't even know

I think the story of Folie à Deux is only made alive because Luc doesn t love Chloé back. She wouldn t have spiraled that much. Her insanity wouldn t have become that dangerous and toxic if he had ever loved her back. But, the most important thing is, you can t force someone to love you. She failed to move on, that s why the story kept going like that. She couldn t let him go.

one day
will be the last day
I will write some
last words for you
this will be the day
my feelings will die
for you
and I do anything
to keep them alive

you will never know
how often I hoped
that you had
someone else
by your side
someone else
waiting for you
so I could
finally stop believing
that we were meant to be
I believed
I was the person
you needed
because you were
the one
I needed the most
I believe
that perfect things
don't exist
if this connection
can't be real

red threads on my head
I look in the mirror

I remind myself of him
he reminds me of myself

I stand in the aisle looking for hair dye
blonde
I want to be someone else so bad

someone died and I got saved

I wanted that Chloé killed someone for Luc to metaphorically show how far obsession and delusion could go and how dangerously it may end. It s symbolical that she killed Victor. She felt like she needed to give him up, like a sacrifice to be together with Luc again. A symbol for a new beginning. A symbol of violently breaking a never ending cycle. Someone dies and something else is coming to life.

folie à deux
je suis folle de toi
je suis folle pour toi

what if
my path
and my
hopes were
also just
lies I
told to
myself you
will never
know me
never see
me never
notice me
never talk
to me
that you
could love
me back
was an
illusion but
my feelings
and all
the things
that I
have achieved
never were

if you
were really
meant for
me
you
would come
back to
me
wherever
I am
you would
literally leave
the stage
and come
to me

you are the sun
I see you shining on your own
I am jealous of your light
only at night
they see me shining
in the night sky
the light is yours
I am the moon

they see me shining in the night sky
but the light is yours

Writing Folie à Deux saved me from losing my mind. I could put everything on paper what I wanted to say, what I wanted to share and wrapping it in a fictional story. The whole story is invented. But if you look closer, the one or the other thing may remind you of me. Chloé is maybe a part of me and I am a part of Chloé. She is my shadow and I am her light. She is embodying everything I never liked about myself: obsession to someone you can t have, ingratitude, putting people on a pedestal, escapism, loneliness, jealousy. Writing about Chloé helped me embracing my shadow, working on myself and coping with my obsessions. I could put it all into words until nothing was left to say.

another sip
white wine
until everything is turning
and everything is turning funny
and I forget my sadness
I stumble into the bathroom
looking at my drunk eyes
in the mirror
and I start laughing
I am going to see him
for the first and last time
I can t enjoy it sober
when I am numb inside
I was waiting
for this moment
and I feel nothing
I don t know
where the floor is
and the ceiling
like reality and dream
are blending

I miss
my past self
it was the day
I was the happiest
and the saddest
lantern lights
on the streets
guiding me
to you
every step I take
is bringing me
closer to you
I don't know
if I miss
seeing you
or if I miss
the false hopes
guiding me
to you

loving you

        felt like loving myself

hating you

        felt like hating myself

letting you go

        felt like letting myself go

reading about you

        felt like understanding myself

I didn't look for answers

        the answers were looking for me

making art

        felt like being closer to you

so if you are an illusion

        does it mean I am an illusion, too?

he didn t even see you
you know that you are replaceable for him
and you really believed you had a chance?
you know exactly that he will never notice you
there are so many out there like you
no, you don't get it
he was there
when I needed him the most
he was there
and now he is gone
but he gave me everything
I ever wanted
I am someone
I always wanted to be
because of him
wake up from your fantasy
it's not real
it's in my head
just a story I invented
when will you finally understand
that you will never be together with him?
her words hurt more
than the pain on my skin
the doctors were right
I was incurably ill
and no pills could help me
ten years ago was the first time
I wanted to die
I was so unbearably sad
it's normal, they said
a small phase during puberty
do you really think it's normal
being so tired
you don't even want to live anymore
so you rather want to discover death instead
because there is no reason to stay
just excuses

I was thirteen years old
and my biggest wish was to die
I wanted help but now it's too late
why should I get help
if I am living a perfect life
in my own little fantasy world?
please let me dream a little longer
I needed so many years to build it
I don't want to wake up
I was looking at the window
the weather was nice
and I hated my life
I just wanted to be dead
not because I am tired
but because of despair
what will happen to me now
what's going to happen next?
why should I keep living
if I am battling an incurable illness
I am delusional
but I say
'they are delusional for hoping
that I get better one day'
and secretly, I prayed for a miracle
and he was there
when I wanted to end everything
when I planned to
say goodbye to everything
yes, I was invisible for him
but this moment meant the world to me
before my my world fell apart
I was nothing
he was my everything
and since then
we don't talk about him anymore

the light is shining on him on me on us

I had visions in my head of a concert. I wanted that the story started there and keeps going. And my own story ended at a concert.

I didn t want that it started with Chloé, it all starts with Luc, her idol and it ends with Luc to emphasise how important and dominant he is in her life as if her world only revolves around him. And Chloé's feelings, her mood, her self worth is dependent on him.

it was the first time
I saw him in real life
up there on the stage
I sing along
and our voices merge
yes, he is real
and we are breathing the same air
I can't see him
only through my phone display
and he is totally not like me
he is so much better than me
I am so endlessly ashamed
that I really believed
that I had a chance
so ashamed
I don't want to return
I don't want to wake up again

and he passes me by
the glitter on his clothes
twinkling at me
the ones that used to blind me
I stretch my arm
I try to touch but I fail
as if he was a hologram

I wanna bury myself here
with a shovel
digging a hole here
in the middle of the concert hall

he will go away
he stopped
standing next to me
as if he read my thoughts

he is real
the artist I have admired
for so long

he is not just a picture
on my phone
so close to me
and he is more beautiful
than on those retouched
and edited photos on the internet

the light is shining on him
on me
on us

I am seeing a green eye
where's the other one?
I guess it's looking at me
everything gets dark
and everything glitters
as if I am dissolving
as if he is only half here
and I am the other half
I wanted to die
and here I am dying
that's how it feels

I wanted to die
I am having a rebirth instead
look at me
please look at me
I'm here
don't you recognise me?
I am your biggest fan
and you don't even know

I was travelling for seven hours
totally worth it
I was suffering for four years
totally worth it
now I am driving home
on a rainy day
old me died in the concert hall

now I am seeing videos of him
talking about suicide
about a goodbye letter of a fan
someone died and I got saved
so if that one thing hadn't happened
I wouldn't have been here
writing these lines
he would have talked about me instead
now I feel alive for the first time

I know we will never be together
in this lifetime
but it is certain
that he wouldn't have ever wanted me
to leave

maybe he saw me
I will never know it
but the most important thing is
that I finally felt seen
by myself

then
I tried to fall
asleep
it didn t work
I closed my eyes
I saw him
standing
in front of me
and I flinched
then disappeared into
dreamless sleep
I woke up
with a racing heart
alone in the dark
hotel room
I saw him yesterday
and now
it s over

folie à 2
(aftermath)

the characters visited me
on a random day
I haven't seen it coming
then I got used to them so easily
nothing stays forever
and now the time has come for them to leave
but Chloé stayed the longest

did you know that love and hate
is coming from the same source?
that's how I feel about her
and all the other characters
they all embody all the things
I hate about myself
but I know they are all part of me
and maybe you identify yourself with them, too
it's human to recognise your flaws
we all carry light and shadow in ourselves
we need to balance
and take care of exaggeration

Chloé reads my stories
she takes her scissors
cuts the paragraphs
rearranges them
and glues them together
in a collage
like a photo album full of words
creating a whole new plot
an invented story
but every line
has a little part of truth

I am not Chloé
I am my own muse

I made it out
she didn't

maybe it was all me
maybe it was just Chloé

I needed to remember
what I wanted to forget

I needed to become her
to tell you her story